Contents

Some words are shown in bold, **like this**.
You can find them in the glossary on page 23.

What is a Gila monster?

A Gila monster is a lizard.

You say Gila as "HEE-la".

Gila monsters belong to a group of animals called **reptiles**.

Crocodiles and snakes are also reptiles.

Where do Gila monsters live?

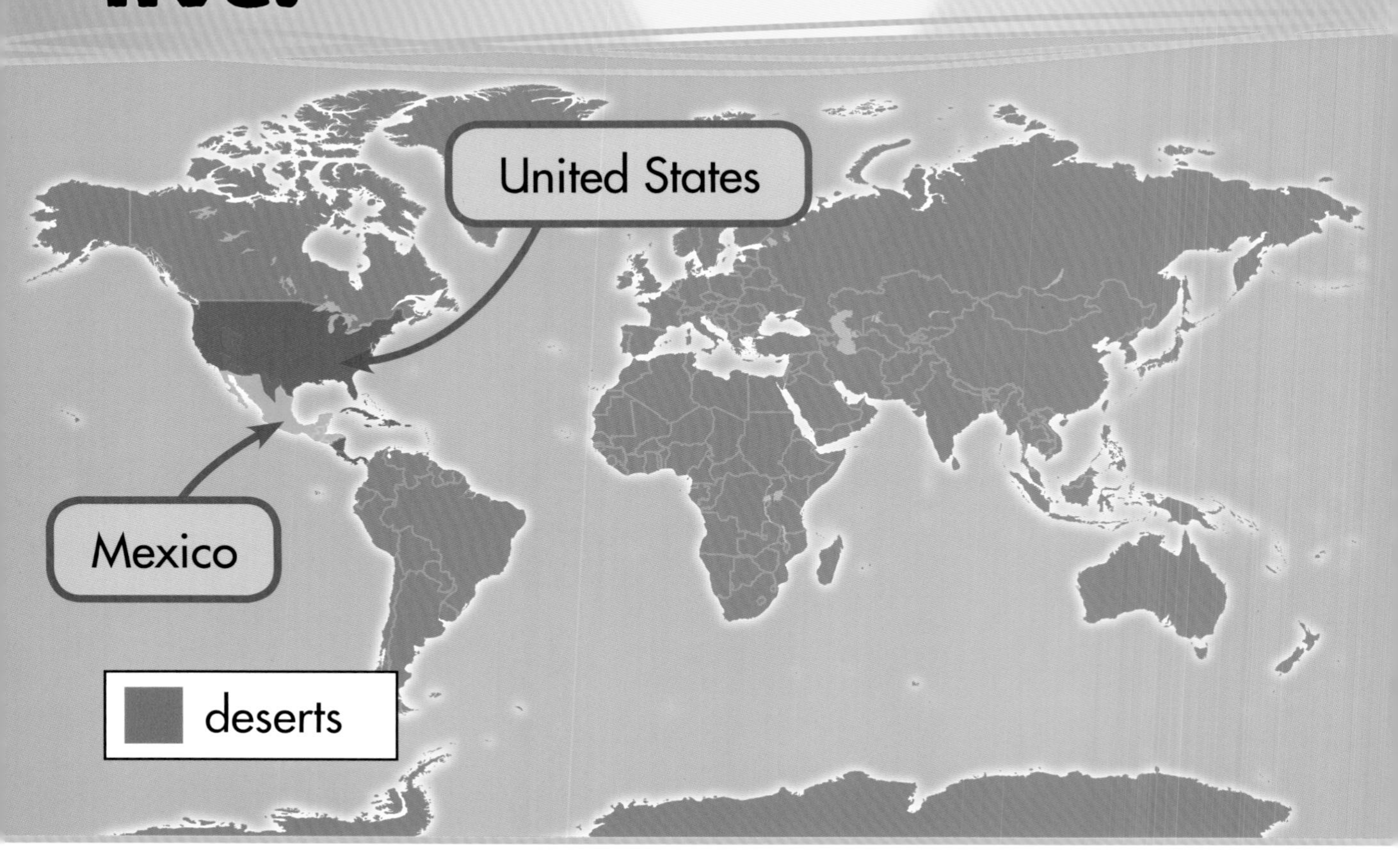

Gila monsters live in the **deserts** of the south-west United States and northern Mexico.

Can you find these deserts on the map?

In the day, it is hot in the desert but it gets cooler at night.

Gila monsters dig **burrows** in the sand or live in burrows dug by other animals.

What do Gila monsters look like?

Gila monsters have big, heavy bodies, with short, fat tails.

They can grow to be as long as your arm.

A Gila monster's body is covered in black, pink, and yellow **scales**.

The scales look like small, round beads.

What do Gila monsters do in the day?

In spring, the weather is cooler in the **desert**.

Gila monsters spend most of the day looking for food.

In summer, it is very hot during the day.

Gila monsters stay in their **burrows** out of the sun.

What do Gila monsters do at night?

In spring, Gila monsters spend the night resting in their **burrows**.

They come out in the morning to go hunting again.

In summer, it is cooler in the **desert** at night.

Gila monsters come out at night to look for food.

What do Gila monsters eat?

Gila monsters use smell to find their food, by flicking their tongues in and out.

They eat birds, eggs, mice, **insects**, and other lizards.

A Gila monster bites its **prey** with its powerful jaws to kill it.

Then the Gila monster swallows it whole.

How do Gila monsters defend themselves?

If Gila monsters are out in the day or night, they have to watch out for **predators**.

Coyotes, hawks, dogs, and wild cats hunt Gila monsters.

If a predator comes close, the Gila monster opens its mouth and hisses.

Then it bites and chews its **poison** into its attacker.

Where are baby Gila monsters born?

In summer, the female digs a hole in the ground and lays her eggs in it.

She buries them and goes away.

Next spring, the eggs hatch and the babies crawl out.

They look like little adults and can already look after themselves.

What do Gila monsters do in winter?

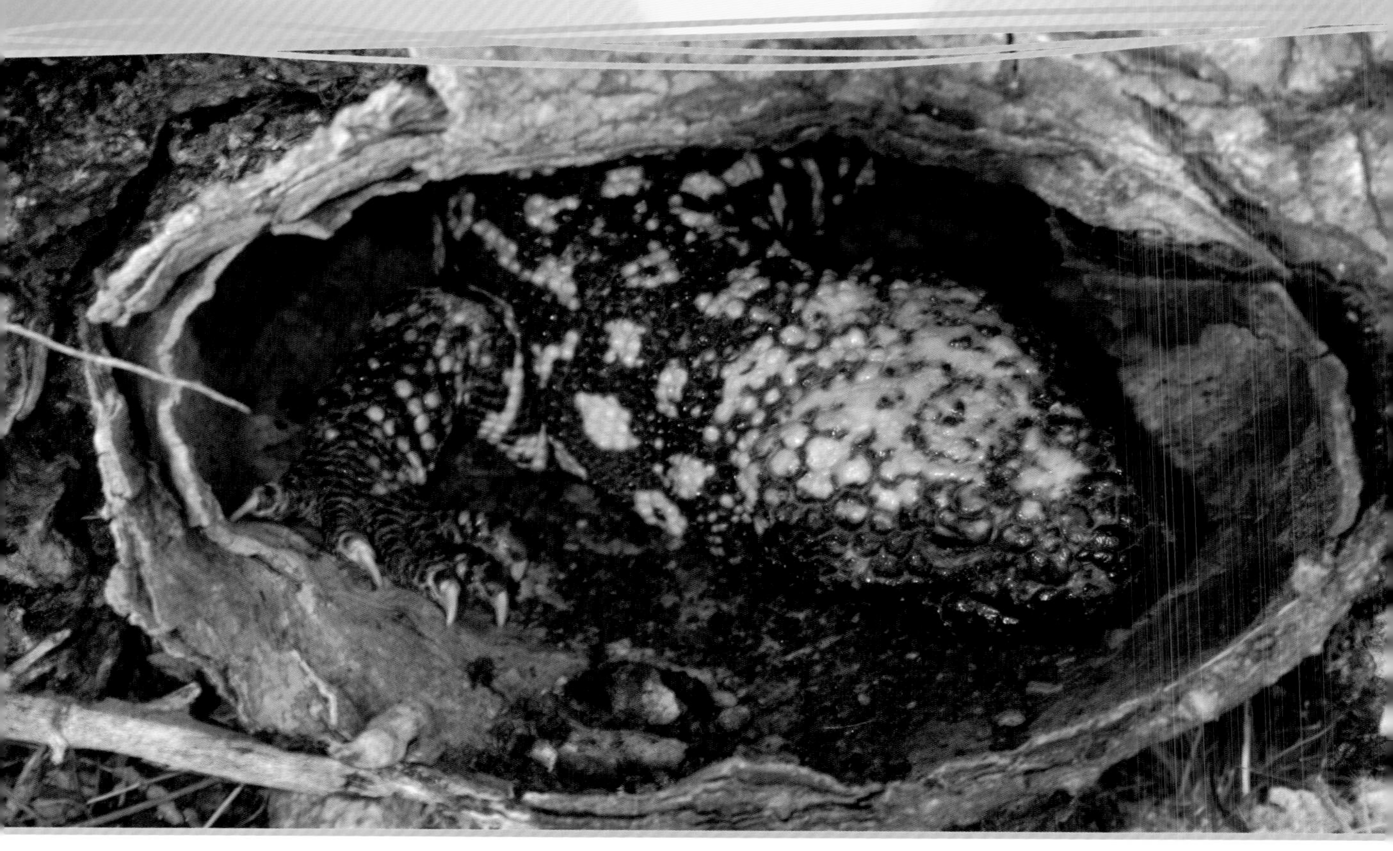

In winter, it gets cold in the **desert**.

Gila monsters stay in their **burrows** and go into a deep sleep.

The Gila monsters do not need to eat in winter.

They live off fat stored in their tails until they wake up again next spring.

Gila monster body map

Glossary

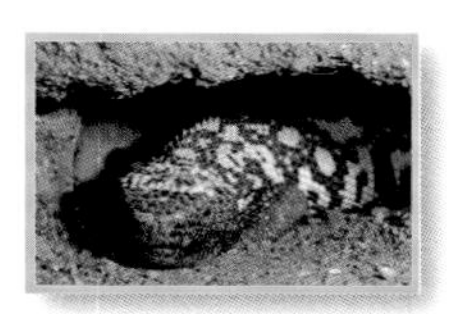

burrow hole in the ground where an animal lives

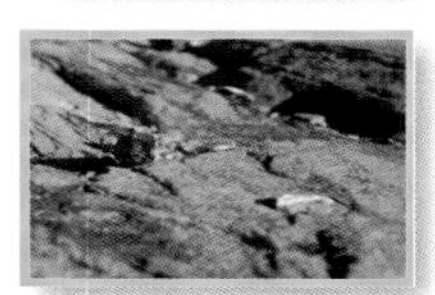

desert very dry place that is rocky, stony, or sandy

insect animal that has six legs, such as a grasshopper

poison something that can cause illness or death

predator animal that hunts other animals for food

prey animal that is eaten by other animals

reptile animal with scaly skin, such as a lizard or snake

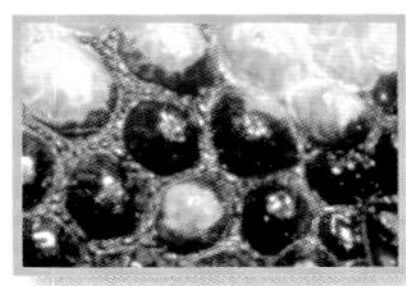

scales tiny flaps of hard skin on a reptile's body

Find out more

Books

Desert Animals (Focus on Habitats), Stephen Savage (Wayland, 2006)

Deserts (My World of Geography), Angela Royston (Heinemann Library, 2004)

24 Hours: Desert (Focus on Habitats), Elizabeth Haldane (Dorling Kindersley, 2006)

Websites

Learn more about Gila monsters at:
kids.yahoo.com/animals/reptiles/4420--Gila+Monster

Look at photos of Gila monsters and find out about them at:
www.sandiegozoo.org/animalbytes/t-gila_monster.html

Index

www.raintreepublishers.co.uk
Visit our website to find out more information about Raintree books.

To order:
Phone 0845 6044371
Fax +44 (0) 1865 312263
Email myorders@raintreepublishers.co.uk

Customers from outside the UK please telephone +44 1865 312262

Raintree is an imprint of Capstone Global Library Limited, a company incorporated in England and Wales having its registered office at 7 Pilgrim Street, London, EC4V 6LB – Registered company number: 6695582

First published in hardback in 2011
First published in paperback in 2012
The moral rights of the proprietor have been asserted.

Edited by Daniel Nunn, Rebecca Rissman, and Sian Smith
Designed by Richard Parker
Picture research by Elizabeth Alexander
Production by Victoria Fitzgerald
Originated by Capstone Global Library Ltd
Printed and bound in China by South China Printing Company Ltd

ISBN 978 1 406 21962 3 (hardback)
14 13 12 11 10
10 9 8 7 6 5 4 3 2 1

ISBN 978 1 406 22125 1 (paperback)
15 14 13 12
10 9 8 7 6 5 4 3 2 1

British Library Cataloguing in Publication Data
Ganeri, Anita, 1961-
Gila monster. -- (A day in the life. Desert animals)
1. Gila monster--Juvenile literature.
I. Title II. Series
597.9'5952-dc22

Acknowledgements
We would like to thank the following for permission to reproduce photographs: Alamy pp. 7, 23 glossary desert (© Andrew Harrington), 8 (© Design Pics Inc.), 12 (© Roberto Nistri), 10 (© Rick & Nora Bowers); Corbis pp. 17, 23 glossary poison (© Kennan Ward); FLPA p. 14 (© ZSSD/Minden Pictures); Getty Images pp. 16 (Barbara Jordan/Photographer's Choice), 18, 21 (Jim Merli/Visuals Unlimited); © Jack Goldfarb p. 22; Photolibrary pp. 4, 9, 20, 23 glossary scales (John Cancalosi/age fotostock), 13 (Matt Meadows/Peter Arnold Images), 11, 23 glossary burrow (C. Allan Morgan/Peter Arnold Images), 15, 23 glossary predator (Marty Cordano/OSF), 19 (PAUL FREED/Animals Animals); Shutterstock pp. 5, 23 glossary reptile (© Susan Flashman), 23 glossary insect (© Anke van Wyk), 23 glossary prey (© EcoPrint).

Front cover photograph of an adult Gila monster (Heloderma suspectum) basking at the mouth of its den reproduced with permission of Photolibrary (Wayne Lynch/All Canada Photos).

Back cover photograph of (left) a Gila monster's scales reproduced with permission of Photolibrary (John Cancalosi/age fotostock); and (right) a Gila monster somewhere in southwestern North America, CA reproduced with permission of Corbis (© Kennan Ward).

The publisher would like to thank Michael Bright for his assistance in the preparation of this book.

A Day in the Life: Desert Animals

Gila Monster

Anita Ganeri